G000060791

Affection & Other Accidents

Poems **Dami Ajayi**

Cover Art: Bridge Partners, 2018 by Sor Sen
Cover Design: Daniel Alberto Flagel
Author Portrait: Yemisi Aribisala

First published in 2022 by
RADI8 LTD.
46, Adebayo Mokuolu Street,
Anthony Village, Lagos.

PRAISE FOR
AFFECTION & OTHER ACCIDENTS

Affection & Other Accidents distills pain in such lucid, understated, but affecting tones to reflect the vulnerability and brokenness underlying human intimacy. A wrenching collection.

— Uchechukwu Peter Umezurike, author of *Double Wahala, Double Trouble*

I don't remember the last time I was so enthralled by and embedded in a waning love affair. Dami Ajayi's lyricism is perfect.

— Yemisi Aribisala, author of *Longthroat Memoirs*

In his third and most alluring collection, Dami Ajayi sheds off the toga of the essential lyricists (Clinical Blues), the gait of the elegant pedestrian (A Woman's Body is a Country) to assume the role of a bohemian existentialist. This is Nietzsche wearing the spectacles of Freud. How the poet manages to tell us about a man walking on carpet of spiky thorns as though it were a peacock pluming in a garden is both surprising and perplexing. Imbued with hurtful memories, skilful stringing of musical chords disguised as consolatory philosophy, Affection & Other Accidents has taken its exclusive space among the most engaging collections in contemporary poetry.

— Umar Abubakar Sidi, author of *The Poet of Dust*

With experimentation with form, Àjàyí here presents another view of his talents as a sculptor of words, even when they carry welts of pain.

— Kọ́lá Túbọ̀sún, author of *Edwardsville by Heart*

DEDICATION

To the Olaleres. Thanks for Sheffield.

ACKNOWLEDGEMENTS

Profound thanks to the editors and staff of the following publications where some of these poems have appeared or are forthcoming:

"Queens", *"Sleeping Beauty (of Borehamwood)"*, *"Waterstones"*, *"Ode to a Face Mask"*, *"Denouement"* in the forthcoming Relations Anthology edited by Nana Ekua Brew-Hammond.

"Codeine Diet" in Nantygreens.

"Aubade to my Greying" in the Memento: Anthology of Contemporary Nigerian Poetry edited by Adedayo Agarau.

"The Anatomy of Silence", *"A Poem for the Condemned Poet"*, *"Untitled"* & *"328 to World's End"* in Lolwe.

"Introit", *"Affection & Other Accidents"* & *"This Academy Called Life"* appeared in NiedernGasse, translated to Italian by Elisa Audino .

Special thanks to Rotimi Babatunde for looking through this manuscript. Tunji Olalere, Feyisayo Adeyemi, Tosin Gbogi, Yemisi Aribisala, Adeola Opeyemi & Socrates Mbamalu – thanks for your thoughtful comments & suggestions.
Thanks Gbenga & Lolade Ajayi for Borehamwood. Victoria Namabiri, I see you LW. & to everyone with a kind word to spare through those difficult times, I am grateful.

Dami Ajayi
London, 2021.

CONTENTS

INTROIT

Bless up
to the variations of diarrhoea
to which I now say amen.

AFFECTION & OTHER ACCIDENTS

I.

A perfect beginning: driving down the Third Mainland Bridge at top speed, loyal friend in the passenger seat hyping, an engagement ring sitting in a box between us, racing against time. But beginnings are hardly rom-com perfect, not in retrospect. I was driving down the bridge *alright*, heading home to you. There was an engagement ring too, a replacement, & time was against us. You had a flight to catch & last night, you had shown a vulnerable side & earned a massive hangover. It was your last day in Lagos & your work colleagues arranged a leaving do. It was in a plush apartment in Victoria Island, the kind that rents for top expat dollars. Culture movers & shakers in attendance, those full of clever things to say about mundane things like tuna sandwich. Alcohol & pastries were in excess, but there was not enough meat. You made several speeches. I thought you were rather chatty, but I imagined you were making an exception for your final night in Lagos. The party wound down; the crowd thinned out. Then you delivered an intimate speech about us, about getting engaged, about your missing engagement ring, about your unfaltering devotion to me & our aisle-bound affection & somehow, somehow, I found myself again kinking one knee, asking for your hand in marriage *again*. We have been here before. Not once. Seven months earlier. I took you to your favourite city & as the day broke in that bougie neighbourhood, in that borrowed room, I went on both knees & asked you to marry me. *Both knees*. Before this, there had been the gold waist chain, a replacement for your metaphorical waist beads that I once destroyed in a poem. Then there was the dream, Josephine, of you wearing an engagement ring, which cancelled your reservation for the promise of marriage with rings. One dream later, you were sold. Yes, you said, yes, then we waltzed to feast. Again, I was on my knee, this time on a borrowed rug. Against the perfect backdrop of a bookcase, I was compelled to ask you to marry me again, this time for the public eye. This time, for the third time, with a borrowed gold ring that fit. The next morning, you were sleeping off your hangover when I left the house in search of a replacement for the ring you had lost barely three months after I slid it into your finger. I found the exact replica with five stones on the other side of Lagos. I knelt once again in the hallowed privacy of our room & placed it in your finger, a perfect parting gift.

II.

You picked the best place to have an argument. A train coach
heading from Berlin to Cologne. You picked the best time too.
The quiet time before travelers eased into siesta. You picked
the best topic. But a black man & a black woman with a white
audience observing their heated conversation? What spurred
that appetite for public spectacle? Earlier that day in Berlin,
we were sharing prosecco with friends & you began to spill my
secrets in a trivial debate. Was it in trade for banter or was it
to look woke? What is the use of an argument that targets our
relationship? What is the use of -isms in this devotion, anyway?
But in that train car, your voice was rising & rising. The other
passengers were becoming uncomfortable. I asked you to make
your argument calmly, but you raised your voice all the more.
Bless the woman who stood from her seat to remind us that
this space was not as private or as hallowed as we imagined. One
hour into that conversation, sleep-deprived & anxiety-stricken,
I began to have a panic attack. My heart pounding against my
chest, I wanted to do two things. One was to get off & never see
you again. Two was to call my mother & apologise for being rude
to her when she began to ask questions about Denmark. & you
kept going at it. This argument for which you must hold the
final word. I thought it will be a civil conversation about how to
love each other in public, about how to disagree in public & still
be civil about it, but you kept hacking at everybody's impatience
on that train ride. I looked out of the racing window, at the
racing, summery German countryside. We were to be married
that summer. A perfect Danish wedding with all your family &
friends & none of mine.

III.

I risked it all to come to India, incredible India. It was a squeeze, the chaos of visa interviews & schedules, but I took those risks because love does. Love endures. Love is relentless. Love trudges. But, most importantly, love asks questions. I risked it all to come to India, to hear your story, to understand how our love was evolving, where our devotion was faltering. You were at the Arrivals waiting with a worn smile. I was loaded with suitcases of your favourite contraband—locust beans, dried fish, dried ewedu leaves, fiery ground pepper. I lingered with questions, but you dismissed them with a tentative smile, with faux warmth, with a hospitality soon to be replaced with hostility. Yet, I lingered with questions. The annual leave days came to an end & you returned to your daily routine. I became an appendage in your house, that guest who might have overstayed his welcome. Yet, I lingered with questions. What happened in that train? I am not a perfect. My past loops into the present, a trail of dalliances returning like the proverbial abiku. I like my strays picked out with flair. I like to play messiah & shaman. Spill myself out for others, empathy on overdrive. These were pastimes that pinch you. I am not a perfect man, but I am earnest. Earnestness did not seem to meet your requirements. Honesty also did not meet your specifications. You had to find things for yourself. The sleuth who loses sleep to unearth secrets on my gadgets. You read my private messages to friends & acquaintances, quizzed me about other people's life choices, sometimes punished me for those choices. There were exes that lingered & loitered, this confirmed your brazing suspicions, even when I said to you that I have shut those doors, you continued to probe & poke old wounds, willing them to bleed. I was not a perfect man, but I was earnest. That was why I came to India, to see if there was any love left, anything we could work with to bring our affection back to speed. But it took only days for your hospitality to sour. The Colony House Rules arrived in spurts. Do not leave the light bulbs on. Do not leave skid marks on the porcelain. Do not leave used plates in the kitchen sink. Do not play music too loud. Do not sit. Do not write at night. Do not ask me questions. I was waiting with questions, waiting for your answers, but we would not speak of Lagos, of Berlin, of Cologne. On the night before I left, we sat on opposite sides of the soft mattress thrown on the floor & argued about marital roles. We argued bitterly about marital roles. Yet my questions lingered, unanswered.

IV.

I left London for the weekend to seek refuge in Sheffield, in the company of trusted friends. London had begun to undo me, I was coming apart. I couldn't seem to do anything right. I couldn't find my way around the tubes. I couldn't understand what this new job entails. At night, I lay in an uncomfortable couch in southeast London, willing sleep to come, watching the ticking clock till dawn. The day arrives & I am already exhausted. But I trudge on. The Thameslink National Rail to Elephant & Castle. The Bakerloo line to Warwick Avenue. Then a thirty minute walk to Maida Hill. On the first day of work, I dressed in a sport jacket & a deluge drenched me. On the second day of work, I slid & fell on Sunderland Avenue. On the third day of work, I tripped on the underground station & fell. I sat on the floor with my overtly yellow luggage & wept. A grown man shedding tears in the Elephant & Castle underground station. I think you could have done better. Put your five-hour head start in New Delhi to good use. Ask how my day went like lovers do in those songs. I believe these things are real, that people check on their lovers even in long distance relationships. The text as replacement for love missives that are written with care, in cursive, making deep incursions into the life of your significant other. The voice message & a keen gift of narration means I could tell you about my day, a very long day that began with being drenched in the rain & spending my afternoon lost because I took Bus 18 in the wrong direction. I was heading to Baker Street, but I took the 18 to Sudbury instead & ended up in Wembley. I fight the afternoon somnolence by going to banks, trying to open a bank account without a letter of introduction. I asked you & you were a quiver, full of excuses. But the most staggering excuse was that indulgent Swedish massage. You were having the time of your life, being kneaded in your plush apartment while I was tracking down the underground stairwell on my buttocks. & there were no buts, no pity, no sympathy. After all, you had already declared that I was incapable of living in Europe.

V.

You broke the silence & came to London. You left instructions to meet you at St Pancras, perhaps you expected flowers too. Expected petals to be dropped on the floor for you to trample upon. Petals like my pride already worn from your footwork. Petals like my love & resolve that had become threadbare. You expected a hero's welcome, perhaps hoped for a lover's welcome, but that ship had already sailed. You came to me with all of your pride & some excuses & you sat in the front room & told me you were here to apologise, not to beg. I think about semantics, about lexicon, about grammar, about intentions, about the subtleties of language. How do you apologise without begging? How does begging differ from apologising? Perhaps begging is a more tortured sight. Begging requires more than being contrite, being full of vulnerable gestures. Grovelling, maybe? But apologising, on the other hand, is formal & officious. It feels like a handshake & keeps dignity intact. You can apologise without breaking sweat. You can apologise cross-legged. You can apologise with a chip on your shoulder, with a plume of smoke issuing out of your mouth. You can apologise without begging. You came to London to apologise without begging—& yet, I chose to accept your apology. I remember that evening in Motel One Berlin, sharing prosecco & being merry, I knew that our affection sank that night. I remember the afternoon in the train to Cologne, I knew that our affection sank that afternoon. The day you wrote me that you knew I was vulnerable in Cologne & you couldn't bear to support me, our affection sank that afternoon. I remembered that humid night in New Delhi, lying opposite each other & arguing about marital roles. Our affection sunk to a new low too that night. & when the Uber came to get me to the airport, that hug we shared did not linger. You quickly walked back into your Colony House without waiting for the final trail of my disappearance.

INTERLOGUE I

Three years &
four proposals later
we stand annulled,
a premarital divorce.

AUBADE TO MY GREYING

I imagined it differently:
toddler daughter pruning my facial garden
notices a speck
& says, "Daddy see."

But my progenies don't breathe air;
they sit on shelves
& I wear
proudly the badge "Author."

My mother & her friends haven't lost hope:
prayers & match-making,
winks & wishing but my dreams rest
on different pastures.
I forage for
a different kind of affection.

& my body is becoming its own thing.
On my watch, a beer gut morphs.
My hairy paunch becomes a shimmering thing
like my inner thigh.

If I were God,
I would do it differently.
Grant those who pray for beards, breasts & buttocks
their dream bodies.

YOUTH

(after King Sunny Adé)

Before apothecaries came
Osun fortified her sons
in a frothy spring of herbs.

In our youth,
we sow our wild oats.
Unlike the sower's parable,
they all fell on loam & flourished
& then there was Cytotec.

Existential angst & peregrinations are
aubades of youth,
the sing-song of mundanity versus
the warmth of random beds in Entebbe, Kigali & Douala.

Lip-stick tainted drawers & throbbing hangovers
incurable by gourmet coffee & aspirin,
the epithet of the moving train
& innumerable stations in its wake.

Now the barren loiter around Osun's riverbanks,
stringing prayers for their loins & almonds
to grow beyond symphyses
into the gravid glory of Beyoncé in radiant yellow,
camwood chalk adorning her face,
sheabutter luxuriating her multi-million-dollar skin.

QUEENS
(after Patrice)

To the Queens of my nickel days,
days blurred by memory's stain.

To the Queens of my jackal days,
days landscaped by sepia dreams.

To the Queens of my Lagos nights,
days pierced by brass & fast cars.

To the Queens of my liminal nights,
Nairobi nights, Cologne nights, Delhi nights.

Nights restive in their nocturnal shifting,
nights that spill into crayon dawns.

To the Queens of my London days,
days edged like a bet,

days of intense feelings & scarred healings,
days interrupted by squeaky train announcements,

days trembling from denouement,
days hoisted like a painter's easel,

days notched by uncertainties,
days weighted with misery's dram,

days seasoned with searing pain,
days salted with sodium & absinthe,

days beaten by monkey wedding drizzle,
days welded with grief & duty,

days watered with wine & whining,
days stretched thin with longing,

days of microwaved lunches,
days of absent queens & promises,

let love songs pour out of radios &
let lonesome poets sing the karaoke of memories,

audit love songs for love,
audit love songs for soothing words.

SLEEPING BEAUTY
(Of Borehamwood)

Be grateful
when your lover's afternoon snores
segue with Ali & Toumani's guitar strings.

This morning we fought
a small war over toilet rolls
at a Tesco till, our affection
smouldering out of what we have
chosen not to call ourselves.

When the sun sets
you will take your beauty
& a supply of essentials,
out of my grasp
away into the waiting hands
of uncertainty, Covid-19 & a fast train.

WATERSTONES

& when the minstrel's wails filter
into the alcove of your dreams,
listen for the words beneath the wail:

it says, don't close your ears
to the gentle strum of tides,
aiding & abetting destiny.

When chance wheels itself in,
do not reach for scales,
statistics, fantasies or traumatic pasts,
reach inwards for the dove's gentleness
& sit out the gale outside Waterstones.

COVID-19

Virus—who would have thought of it?
Neither fire nor man,
nor sceptre, nor mace,
nor frisson of blond hair
tousled in helicopter blade whirls.

Virus, named for envelopes.
The Global North deserves from the East
missives ferried in spores,
spur of the moment.

A sneeze in the mid-clouds,
& what is given cannot be taken back.
Now, Europe sits wonky,
situation room of the world.

To think that Rome would be crippled again
with viral load
& an African sun will scorch viral particles
even in churches.

The tall world order of irony
is in the black body count.

ODE TO A FACE MASK

Dark, like my skin,
not black, call it beige or brown,
but for its rumpled form
it could have been beautiful.

How lonely it must be,
velvet-brown,
to journey from a cotton farm,
spin through textile machines,
be woven into fabric,
manhandled by a tailor
for this fate of abandonment.

Your fate reminds me of breath
& George Floyd on asphalt,
an American knee weighing
against his neck.

Perhaps this was the notion
that spurred your principal
to tug at your fine velvet
in a survival haste for air hunger.

Nothing is promised,
your immaculate cut,
exquisite stitching,
delicate embroidery
did not promise the warmth
of exhaled air.
Your future is grim & tragic,
lying on the concrete's skin

to be trampled upon by the
insouciant wayfarer.

Nothing is promised,
not even the grip of the
litter picker.

CODEINE DIET

Online is a weak cyber-metaphor for high,
but you already know—
like you know blue is the colour of the sky.
VBO Lounge originals

are Sky Vodka bottles rebranded.
Coquettish pony-tailed waiter,
waist bag thickens her sex appeal,
doing a non-committal *Shaku-Shaku*.

Bishop, in his moment of linguistic epiphany,
deconstructs this dance as demonic Shackle-Shackle

for next Sunday sermon—no thoughts for Mary Mary.
We return to the VBO Lounge, where online is vicious market,
where lonely lovers find fraud thinly disguised as longing;
Yahoo Yahoo is neither reverse colonialism nor slavery redux:
it is humanity revisited.

Somewhere in the psyche ward
a registrar discovers Freud.

INTERLOGUE II

It is still surreal
that you did me dirty
in five cities.

MARY'S IN INDIA
(after Dido)

Mary
the sun will rise &
set on you alone today.

It is certain that you
deserve a thousand good wills
& one reason to be truly happy.

It is certain that you will
one day find that you lost
what your heart longed for the most.

That the pull-push of ambivalence,
the stuttering of indifference,
would have fared better if you
considered a little kindness.

If vulnerability was not to you
the stuff of soiled diapers,
the suppurations of constipated isms.
Mary,
the sun will rise &
set on you alone tomorrow.

When the sorrow
of Cupid's broken arrow
reminds you that love also
leave scar tissues.

But you favoured the analgesia
of conceptual pain
over the healing of an assured
devotion.

Here is to your eternal paraesthesia,
your recurrent allodynia
your persistent paraplegia
in the morbid neurology of
future unrequited loves.

Mary,
the sun will rise &
set on you alone always.

THE WAITING ROOM
(In memoriam Mrs Ojuri)

There are waiting gestures,
pressed on faces
while the mind runs amok.

Outside the waiting room,
people wait because
rooms do not expand.

Inside the waiting room,
everything is pristine
except the minds of those
inhabiting it—& the ones they love.

Minds making matters worse,
imagination doing overtime,
splattering overrated possibilities.

Beware, you may find yourself dwelling on
the wrong statistic, dueling with the wrong
side of statistics.

You may find yourself asking
why this room continues to
exist as though the woman you love
is not between coma & eternal sleep.

UNRELIABLE NARRATOR

Maybe she remembers
maybe she begs to forget
the texture of stolen kisses
taken at hostel car parks
under the canopy of the hatchback,
soft music cooing.

Maybe she begs to forget
or fails to remember
how silence punctuated subtle exploration
& visceral conversations automated
by passion. How pliant lips duel
on borrowed bed spreads,
soft music cooing.

Maybe she fails to forget
or begs to remember
the shade of the nights,
the sour edge of the forbidden.
She would rest her head on
my bony knee & wait for the daybreak,
soft music cooing.

Distance & time distorts,
priorities reshuffle.
The night hasn't changed its
shade & texture much, but people change
& their circumstances too,
soft music cooing.

DECLARATION

There is no rule in the book
that says don't name it
if you feel it
so, here again
I declare to you my
unflinching affection pirouetting
with the ease of happy toddlers
trampling with dainty little feet
in a mid-summer evening.

LIFE GOES DOWN LOW
(after Lijadu Sisters)

Life goes down low
& I am sunken with despair
life goes down low
like the dyspnoeic flame of an oil lamp
flaring for survival
like everyman
limbs buckling from a viral undertow
& birds don't chirp no more
& butterflies do not flutter
& the overcast clouds shield sunlight
& strangers do not offer smiles
from behind dark face masks
& the cold continues to call
& I remember why I left the tropical sunshine
& whenever the cold calls,
I acknowledge my exile
& my new life measured out in
teaspoons of honey & absinthe.

SAY IT

(after John Coltrane)

Picture this:
A rented room in Greater London.
Cheap scented candles drooling wax on a parquet floor
& jazz notes filtering toward the bed where two bodies lie.

Call them lovers & you may be right.
Call them lovers & you may be wrong.
There lies the dilemma—in naming.

But read the room again:
aplomb with muted gestures,
understand the play between arousal & restraint,
between billowing winds & clattering blinds,
tapping odd notes into the Coltrane of our lives.

The night woos the day from the sun,
bodies would melt if only slips become undone.
My hands dance slowly over your back;
in tandem to the rhythm of smoky bluesy notes,
what escapes from your lips could be a drawn-out sigh
or a moan.

TONIGHT

There is a Lupita dancing alone in every nightclub tonight.
Tonight, there are men licking her skin with their eyes
& the DJ who plays Beyoncé.

Tonight, a regular John may empty his beer into his laps
but Lupita will mind her business & whine her waist.

Tonight, another John will find her belly-button ring
in his toy trophy.
But tonight, Lupita will shun everything outside her body;
she will mind her business & whine her waist
as though there is no haste,
as though she made time.

Tonight, Lupita won't thread a needle
for complexion & its complexities.
Tonight, she will sublime her worries
with her waist.

BIG HANDS

Fate's big hands
stretched out for a handshake.
My world quakes from within
& I regard these hands, these lithe fingers,
these acquaintances that linger
with quavering promises.

Fate's big hands again.
A bladder threatens social conventions &
I dally between digits & micturition.
I chose the urinal over your tentative smile.

Fate's big hands again.
Three strikes, one night.
I had folded your memory into
shelves where cobwebs belong.
The night was not young & I had a train & a plane to catch,
I had London summer to navigate with a Samsung & song.
I dropped to the platform & there you were, without a smile.

POLE DANCER
(after JP Clark)

Look at what the young night birthed:
a restless silhouette darting from blind spot
to imaginary to crisp reality.

She ripples southwards on the pole
& unwinds my DNA
& tickles my claustrum
& breaks my moral compass.

Here I am, earthy like Bekederemo,
transfixed by a dancer
not from Agbor,

not from Askamaya,
not from the patch of earth
she trots with her high heels.

She trembles & leaves a quiver
of cupid arrows in my loins.
Agile like a beaver
but fleeting like a Pentecostal church miracle.
She flinches out of reach like
a flint of fantasy,
like Blondy's sweet sweet Fanta Diallo.

INTERLOGUE III

& years later
ellipsis becomes elision
becomes a dot becomes
a blinking cursor
beginning to blur.

SHOE STRINGS

Of all things to filch
you chose shoestrings,
perhaps because you
don't get the mechanics of it:
how something so flimsy—
how an aglet could hold
the entire weight of a boot.

But if I were you, I would have
pilfered a column of good books,
but where is the good head?

Where is the patience to dwell
on sentences poised to shapen your life?
Where are the exotic cuisine,
platters of pasta & proposed writing,
dessert?

Of all things to filch
you chose shoestrings.

CANCELLING R. KELLY

I know lust at first sight,
eyes meeting before lips
lips meeting before bodies
bodies meeting before silm
soils orange bedspreads,
leaving a patch shaped like the map of
a raunchy memory.

Wee hours & a kissing session,
getting blown by
soft winds rustling through gaping balcony doors
the din of nightlife ferries in heated prayers,
competing with the cooing noughties playlist
to which R. Kelly's voice segues in.

You disrupt pleasure to shut off the music.
You will not fuck me to a R. Kelly tune.
I slouch in awe, perplexed & wooden
with desire. I imagine politically correct
ways to put you back into my bed, in zone
to resume our Bump & Grind shenanigans.

Moments later,
we sit at the balcony,
at ease wearing only our joints,
sipping coffee & watching the day break,
at dawn, you don't thank me
& say bye-bye.

THE BODY KNOWS

The body knows
the machinations of the mind
the ladies you swiftly undress
in the haze of the sun
between ward rounds &
warm evenings,
the lovers you may have taken
if this love won't come undone
the body knows,

it knows
when a greeting lingers on the tongue tip,
the lick of your lip corners,
the bleat in your eyes
when a beauty saunters into the room—
the danger of looking twice,
the body knows,

it knows
that flesh is weak
& the mind is sick
& fantasies are electric
& passion is for those who seek
the body knows,

it knows
the cadence of pounding pestles
& the nudge of camaraderie,
it knows the licks of salty backs
& the scent of silm
the body knows

it knows
the murk of monogamy
& the unbridled passion of the novelty
it seeks.

THE CRUCIBLE
(for Chebet)

We let the logistics of saying goodbye
overwhelm us, like young lovers.

We remain tentative
although we meant to be spontaneous.

With ethanol & laughter & the canopy of night
we feasted on music & our bodies,
whispers into ossicles tickle
when you contend with booming Hi-Fis
when you have recused this affection.

In the melee of a night
between lover's rock & rocksteady
you told me of your future
waiting in a small town in America,
then you pause, auditing my slow uptake,
I sigh & quash my cigarette in the crucible,
stay my gaze by watching hands & mouths,
the furtive journey of chewing khat,
familiar to this turn of phrase.

Nothing was promised:
neither the abject pain of departure,
nor the sting of cheap gin
slicking down throats.

The photophobia of hangovers persists
at the departure bay
& your frantic voice notes,
in lieu of a goodbye.

A GHAZAL FOR MY INNOCENCE

I once asked my father how children came about. He looked
into my eyes & said,
your mother & I prayed

so that night, I knelt by my bedside & asked
to be gifted with a sib,
I prayed

between role-playing with my peers
& being fondled by Auntie Sheri's furtive fingers,
I prayed

laid hands on my mother's tummy & praying it erupts
like Mummy Sharon's belly, even though father was away,
I prayed,

my innocence brow-beaten by my mother's paranoia
& her wavering trust of neighbours,
I prayed;

innocence veiled by a gossamer of ignorance,
I knew coitus only by its native name,
yet I prayed

with the conviction of a child's well-fed delusion,
mother's love diminishing with father's seasonal return,
still I prayed

till science taught me about sex & procreation
& contraception & the positions couples assume
when they prayed.

A PANTOUM FOR GABRIEL

(to be accompanied with drums)

Let a poem ferry you, ancestor
to the hereafter
across the River Nun
to pearly gates & things promised.

To the hereafter
where beauty is song
to pearly gates & things promised
where the body becomes eternal.

where beauty is song
across the River Nun
where the body becomes eternal
let a poem ferry you, ancestor.

FUNERAL DRESSINGS

At my great grandmother's funeral,
her remains laid in state.
It was a performance to my four-year-old mind—
no drab house clothing sun-dried by camphor.

My nan was dressed
like an English bride with white platform shoes,
perhaps to irk her long-gone husband
at her second & final wedding.

My grandfather's remains had begun to rot before his final outing.
Dressed in beige aso-oke, his prescient passing was a celebra-
tion of life,
tears shed were libations to placate earth for his smooth jour-
ney to the hereafter.

Ife's coffin was just about the right fit,
his body dressed in his favourite shirt
but someone failed to roll-up his sleeves,
in case of a tyre blowout en route heaven.

Tending to a ward full of comatose patients
snoring their ailing bodies
backward, forward, backward to purgatory,
I missed Tolu's burial
but I wonder if they let him wear dark shades,
as an heaven-bound celebrity.

I will not forgive the mortician who dressed Seyi's body
& wore him white nylon gloves like an antiquated groom,
his wife struggling against the lowering of his body
in his final marriage with mother earth.

THE EXORCISM

I cannot enjoy the alto of Funmi Aragbaiye's music
because Sioni is a different kind of city—

hilly mounds of her mons venus, sparse hair & infected follicles
moist lingerie squeezed in her right hand, like an accordion—

her back, her arching back—desperate gasps
issuing through her broken teeth—
is not all I remember.

Night terrors rocking my growing body—
I must have been four or five or six.
My mother couldn't process the restive sleep,
the groggy sleep-talking,
the unsteady sleep-walking that led my jaw to the bedpost,
ribbons of blood issuing into the maroon bedspread—

I remember church that Thursday evening.
An unmanned drum kit lit by candles aiding the Pastor
exorcising the demon murdering my sleep—

But it was mother who came under, etherized,
skirt hiked, when the unnamed demon fled the nave.

OTHER ROOMS

When the drunk comes home,
disregard his ataxia,
but reward his one-shoed return
with silence & soulless sleep.

Till the cops come calling
on the brothel next-door
& their tethered mongrel becomes
the muezzin's honest mistake at Adhan.

This room is a mundane museum of our mortal existence.
Bed snug to one corner. Windows pouring in light,
dark curtains shutting light out,
your preference.

Two rooms ago,
we shared the cacophony of
estate mechanics at noon
& nights denuded of air,
nights asphyxiated by clattering generators
cha-cha-cha-ing the silence.

Tonight,
dark curtains pour silhouettes
on your bedside &
I tell myself that there
will be other rooms.

A REQUIEM
(for Babalola)

The living have crossed the threshold, stepped into the shoes of those who don't change clothes, those who don't bathe, those who don't fart or burp, those who don't cough or lose weight, those who don't carry wounds, flies & shame alongside their family name. The living can draw a last breath to join the dead. The dead don't preen over social conventions like cavernous nostrils or anterooms for drain flies. The dead do not bother the living about healthy living. The dead don't say. The dead are to those to whom we pray & pour libations. They are better than us—ancestors, whose crooked & knowable paths on earth we measured by our cynicism. They are better than us now. The ones who have crossed the threshold to join the gods to become gods. Yours was an unknowable path. Yours was a life measured out with a teaspoon, on your own terms.

A POEM FOR RALIAT

Wife-in-waiting,
camwood adorning her feet,
her groom, with proverbial blue balls, waiting too.
this love came through serendipity,
the activist found love at the instance of delirious duty.
Good things come, not only to those who wait, but to those
who sigh, unbothered, when promised affection slither out
of reach.
Never mind that.
never mind that affection is a shimmering thing catching
the reflection of a full moon on desperate nights when
lovers deign to dream of an alternate future.
But love knows to navigate destination
& that is how affection gains its form like a foetus.
Affection trudges through memory, through cornerstones,
through conduits forgotten & neglected.
Affection finds itself a stool
in places not foretold
at an Ordinary General Meeting.
Love finds itself & that is enough.
That is enough.

ACNE VULGARIS

Some study the cartography of their faces
for doctorates in vanity.
Look into the mirror,
see what you've become.
We made faces at our mirror reflections
before we invented selfies.
See pustules once swollen,
pregnant with martyred leukocytes & pus.
See blackheads, whiteheads, comedones,
if my dermatology posting still serves.
Rub one of the eighty-four-plus minor monuments
dotting your face.
Time has made an Enwonwu
of your post-pubertal face.
Integuments are entanglements
that do not navigate the soul shuttle.
I see beyond this graffiti of acne
that is your face.

BIRTHDAY ELEGY
(for Pius Adesanmi & Others)

& what poem shall we give
to comfort the child by the windowsill
awaiting her father's impossible return?

What poem shall reinstate the
tentative smile of a husband?

When ephemeral farewells acquire permanence,
poets must shut up
& commit to silence.

But silence is a treacherous thing,
even if it is the nature of words to fail.

Silence is duplicitous.
Silence is complicit,
resigned to fate as a deckhand.
Silence is too fatal an act
for a poet to commit.

A plane stumbled & fell at Bishoftu
on my birthday.
Bodies, blood & blurry memories
redacted the felicity of vain numbering
& here I am, wounded by grief,
contemplating in silence:
Is dying for the dead
as it is for the living?

ON GRIEF

At the end of this reel called life
we must fight difficult departures,
sudden, even if, premeditated.
We pray that the dying that comes
to the ones we love
carry the weight of meaning
& in their prescient passing,
we seek the meaning
of a life beautifully lived
in inconsolable tears,
we anchor fractal memories
we stifle sobs with lofty
aspirations of a lively afterlife.
Even if what remains is cold
& the soul has long crept away
from the grasp of corporeal perceptions.
Grief is what we the living must do.

HOW TO GRIEVE IN TIME

There is no such thing
as to grieve in time
for we cannot teach
grief how to be brief.
But time is balm,
its reassuring calm
comes to those
who put their memories
out at night for the dew,
those who honour
their dead with worship.
Those who place them
in the pantheon of their thoughts,
those who invoke their dead
energise them
with unrelenting memory,
with sentient songs.
Grief, the rocky route,
becomes easier as time passes.

EPITAPH

Show me the tombstone of the man
whose peregrinations aimed to wreck the earth;
the patch of soil above his remains
is in memory of his feeble efforts.

The land & her kin
the oceans & seas
the glaciers & clouds
mountains & hills
will succeed us all.

This earth, though we call it home,
is not our home.

IN PRAISE OF GOD'S STALKER
(after Chief Commander Ebenezer Obey)

Good luck to the man
who appoints himself
God's stalker.
& good luck to his
timeless tomfoolery.

Disquiet & envy stink for days
on end, in vindication of mere merit,
in veneration of the watcher's delusional itinerary.

But I have fled from my enemies
like a bird kites into the sky.

But I have fled from my enemies
like a squirrel scurries into the wild.

But I have fled from my enemies
like a shark shirks away from other sharks.

& the boulder installed to block my path
aided my sweet escape.

INTERLOGUE IV

& what is love without reciprocity:
that boomerang effect,
with the mathematical integrity
that what you have given
is given back?

FIRST STRIKE

Tonight, you found my ire.
You forced the hands of goodwill.
Rising voices betray frayed nerves,
what is the use of anger
if not to dissolve resolve?
If not to throw viscous sputum skywards
& catch it on your face.
Such exhibitionism!
I have tried to digest my doubt
with stowed-away enzymes.
But if this is all of your love,
then my food allergies must be kind.

UNTITLED
(for Chebet)

Grief is a slippery thing.
No loss perfects the act of losing a loved one.
Each loss is different, a new thing.
Dendrites crushed,
heart quivering, mourning forever
the fatality of mortal bodies.

The night before you left
fond thoughts of you poured into
my chalice & I smiled in remembrance
& said a soft prayer for you
without knowing that you were
doing the final round of appearances.

When the cortege returned to say
you had been irretrievably ripped
from us, I shattered in an open office
& held on to fond nocturnal memories
& a song.

It shouldn't have been you
to slip away one spring morning.
I struggle, grappling for totems
to remember you by.

Grief is a slippery but deeply human thing.
I pray for the repose of your soul
& your return to share your beauty
once again with the world.

Bring alligator pepper this time
& the scar from the sting of youthful death
& the utopia of the Yoruba prayer
that days be distant from each other.

FALL

The other day,
a mishap fell me.
I beheld the sky
& it showered rain.

A child falls prone & looks forward,
an adult falls prone & looks backward.

A man falls
& he looks to the sky.
I looked at the sky
& it showered rain.

I looked sideways
& heard footfalls nearby.
But it is not the imperative of strangers
to gather my steps.

I looked again
& I saw my friends,
& their fair-weather smiles.
I looked at the ones I have loved
& they looked away from me.

The world swirls in its misery,
the marketplace devoid of a daily tally
balloons at dawn & shrinks at dusk
in preparedness for the market of the otherworldly.

The night passes without significance
for those who are not troubled.

The day passes without significance
for those who are troubled.

Tell the ground where I fell
that I don't know why I fell
tell the ground that fell me
that the lesson still eludes me.

This earth, a parch of life form,
has an even temper;
why has it chosen to mete out anger to me?

This earth is a patch of life form
with an even temper
why has it chosen me for an example?

The day passes with certainty;
night arrives & the feet that fell at dawn
trudge their weary homeward return.
They pause yet they do not stop.

INTERLOGUE V

"...in the days we spent in Cologne, I felt like I was carrying an extra weight..."

It is stormy inside my tranquil soul. It is summer outside in Cologne & bright & beautiful too. Then a deluge ensues. Two lovers are caught. The rain pelts with vengeance. There are no brollies; no parasols for shelter. See, bodies prepared for tanning damned by the unravelling of the weatherman's assurances. "Baby, will you be my summer rain? Carl Thomas sings the twist to Stevie Wonder's Summer Soft. In the middle of the night, alone. I feel her kisses, my nerve endings anticipating, with haptic relentlessness, the subtle bites, the sadomasochism of her love & then she makes it rain but fails to bring the sun back.

NAKED I AM BEFORE YOU RIVER DUN

Naked I am before you River Dun.
A dunce, damned, done.

Juan Donne,
this valediction doesn't forbid mourning.

Be a man, saith the threshing waters.
Be a man.

Night does not extend itself beyond morning.
Day does not extend itself beyond dusk.

The most tangled knot,
with patience,
becomes undone.

The most adored affection, too,
becomes undone.
& you are not done.

The hangman's rope dangles an option;
it will not be yours to take.

There is love enough to
repair your flailing heart.

There is love enough to
darn your inadequacies.

Keep the night,
lest tomorrow brings the light.

THE ANATOMY OF SILENCE

What do I accept from this silence,
this silence that lacerates peace,
this silence, anathema to bliss.

This silence, pensive, dramatic
amping tension, wrecking intention,
this silence, violent & vicarious,
this silence between two lovers &
two phones.

This silence seems to say something,
my bunny ears cocked at the angle of a
murderous gun,
I can't hear you
I can't hear
I can't.

I listen for silence,
the rub of nappy hair on metal,
the rub of stringy beard on brass.
I listen beyond this silence
to the tragic music of indifference;
if victory invites ululation,
why must silence seek its own company?

I know comfy silence
plush like Persian rugs &
burgundy ottomans,
silence cut with the finesse of
affluence.
Silence that

accounts for itself.
Silence that touches itself.

I know post-coital silence
spent bodies in repose,
the plop of a weary heart
buried so far deep in a rack
of ribs.

I know the silence of old couples
sashaying in the wind,
cloth hems fluttering,
holding hands & each other's lives
with a gentle grip calcified
by church blessings & offspring.

I know the silence of flailing love
Its complacency trudging with egg-shell caution
I know the silence of sibling rivalry,
knotted by mother's love
& cord blood.

I know the silence that precedes sleep.
The dip into unconsciousness,
neurones decelerating,
activating slow waves & dreams

I have learnt the lofty lesson of silence &
its kinship with patience.

The gap between
two songs on a playlist is silence.
The lacuna between two rising voices is silence.

The response to unrequited love is silence.
A mother's call of an errant child demands silence.
The gaps between prayers is silence.
The hallmark of a graveyard is silence.

Tell the tranquil waters about silence
Tell the aftermath of a reverberating echo
about silence.

Tell silence about silence & silence will be
its response. But where do I hold this silence?

A POEM FOR THE CONDEMNED POET

I

The poet is in the dock,
hands in cuffs.
See these manacles
as adornments for affection.

Like Orunmila,
Nothing good comes easy in Iwo.
Nothing good comes easy.
Nothing good comes
when the bailiff sends his vocal cords
on a mission,
when the obese judge's seat squeaks
& the court is in session.

II

Do you know this man?
I do not know this poet.
Have you ever seen him?
No, not in this lifetime.
Does he mean anything to you?
Does he mean anything at all?

The witness is excused.
Lips taut,
hair swept behind a scarf,
lithe fingers, dainty gait,
like a flower in spring.
Feet shod in white sneakers,
eyes accompany her out of the courtroom.

III

What allocutus shall the poet give
for his liberty in the Court of Inquiry
on Affection?

What words shall save him from the
despair of frivolous desire?

In this poem for the condemned,
nothing shall save the poet
from the gauntlet of justice.

Nothing shall be saved,
not even the wreath of a smile.

Nothing is expendable.
The poet will drown &
the witness will be Pontius Pilate,
hands washing water.

328 TO WORLD'S END

I

you know nothing of the *senbene*
of a dying cigarette or friendship

loyalty lapsing,
theatrics of a deflating balloon

a macabre Brownian darting
ends with a flutter & a fall,
the *senbene* of a dying friendship,

the discarding of a cigarette butt,
a slow cure to a perfect life.

In the 328 heading to World's End & Chelsea,
the cold wafts in, for hugs & company,

for friendship that we cannot afford.
The seat next to me is vacant,
so the cold sits & kneads me.

II

night
& the waiting starless sky,
the shrivelling cold too
that reminds an émigré
of home & unanswered prayers

outsourced waterproof warmth from a pullover
does not compare to that of the genial Jamaican lady
explaining her small actions like they matter
to an unlikely stranger.

night
& Fela's horns deign to
pierce the night vicariously
through my ears.

night
& the night soil man
makes peace with his
serfdom.

THE TWINS OF WEMBLEY

You may have encountered them too.
Two black middle-aged men
on Wembley High Road
walking side by side,
portly with the accretions of age,
weathered faces, the visage of sage.

You may spot their striking similarities first,
then their milder differences:
how one is clean shaven &
the other wears a stubble.
They don't smile often.

Science insists that monozygotic twins result
when a zygote cleaves after fertilisation
but cannot explain a lifetime of reparation,
cannot explain their affirmative reconciliation.

But the gods know
that a man or a woman
should not be alone so they privileged
these two, lifelong companions.

The Yoruba know, too,
the beauty of preordained mutualism
& deified the symmetry of twinning
& conjured a myth.

In Igbo-Ora,
every family is blessed
& visited upon by the god of twins,
but science insists that it must be their yams.

Black-eyed beans
slow cooked in red oil suffices,
the Yoruba burst into song,
preening with desire
for double blessings.

I know, too,
of the blessings they bring
as a sib preceding twins—
that privilege
is indeed my biggest win.

DENOUEMENT
(after Derek Walcott)

A time will come
when, with a sigh,
you will exhale.

That evening,
gloomy weather may persist
in a world brimming with Covid disease,
but your heart will rid itself of grief,
fluttering pigeons & embrace ease.

Then you will raise a glass of wine
to your portrait in the gilded mirror,
your favourite songs streaming,
supper stewing on an electric stove

& suddenly your solitude
will be tolerable.

MANUS CARESS
(For T.)

She runs her fingers over my hands
teasing me about how soft & supple my palms are.
Like a lazy man's hands, I ask
& she throws her head back, in laughter.

It is not funny,
not in the logic of matrimony,
ancient & modern(?)—
the man (groom?) provides.

I call her routine manus caress
& she laughs again,
not out of courtesy.
What does it mean, she asks?

Manus, I say, is the Latin word for hand,
distal portion of a mammal's forelimb,
including prehensile fingers, opposable thumbs,
palmar creases,
downy hairs she caresses in the alcove of her car
parked under a streetlamp struggling with sleep.

Jazzy hands, beaded hands, paper-straw-holding hands,
bowling hands, hands that Wande Coal asks to kiss.
In medicine, hands are the body's rear mirrors showing
palmar erythema, finger clubbing & Dupuytren's contracture
styled like the priest's signum crucis, preceding the solemn
call to prayer. Press your hands together. Pray with me.

THIS ACADEMY CALLED LIFE

Old bunnies learn
new tricks all the time
in this academy called life.

In this academy called life
where time is tenure, is tuition,
is teacher, is hallowed lecture theater.

& if time is holy room,
watch me consecrate myself,
watch me strip into God's sameness.

& I pray to time: please be kind this time
keep the ease of this affection,
make it endure the ennui of a lifetime.

About Author:

Dami Ajayi is a Nigerian writer and psychiatrist. He is the author of the poetry chapbook Daybreak & Other Poems (2013). His first volume of poems, Clinical Blues (Write House, 2014), was a finalist of the ANA Poetry Prize. It was also longlisted for the Melita Hume Prize and the Wole Soyinka Prize for Literature. A Woman's Body is a Country (Ouida Books, 2017), his second volume, was selected by Quartz Africa in 2017 as one of the best books of the year, and it was a finalist of the Glenna Luschei Prize. His poems have been translated into Yoruba, Portuguese and Italian.

Printed in Great Britain
by Amazon